Contents

A Spring play   6

Making scenery   8

Decorations and costumes   10

Practising the play   12

The day of the play   14

Performing the play   16

The end of the play   18

Index   20

Notes to parents and teachers   21

We are learning about Spring.

Blossom is on the trees.

We can see the signs of Spring.

Frogspawn is in the pond.

We are learning about Spring.
This is a poster we made for the
wall of our classroom.

My First School Play

Rebecca Hunter

Photography by Chris Fairclough

Evans

First Times
My First Day at School
My First School Play
My New Sister
My First Visit to Hospital
My New Dad
Moving House
My First Pet
My First Visit to London

Published by Evans Brothers Ltd
2A Portman Mansions
Chiltern Street
London W1M 1LE
England

First published in 2000

Hunter, Rebecca
My first school play, - (First Times)
1. College and school drama - Juvenile literature
2. Children's plays - juvenile literature
1. Title
792

ISBN 0 237 52021 4

Acknowledgements
Planning and production by Discovery Books
Editor: Rebecca Hunter
Photographer: Chris Fairclough
Designer: Ian Winton
Consultant: Trevor Jellis M.A., M.Phil., A.F.B.Ps., Psychol. is a Chartered Psychologist who has spent thirty years working with individuals, schools, companies and major corporate institutions in the management of stress. He deals with individuals who are suffering from stress both in their family life and in the workplace.

The publishers would like to thank Zhengchu Tam, Mr and Mrs Tam, Mrs Jaggers and the staff and pupils of Harborne Infants School, Birmingham for their help in the preparation of this book.

We are going to do a play.

My teacher says that we are going to do a Spring play. She asks who would like to be in the play. I put up my hand.

We are making scenery.

The play is about the animals and flowers that appear in Spring.

I am making a daffodil which will be part of the scenery.

I have to learn
a poem.

I have to learn a poem for the
play. My Mum helps me learn it.
It is not too hard.

We decorate the hall.

My friend Katie
helps me put up
the decorations.

I like this picture with the
big, black tadpoles best.

Now it is time to try on our costumes. We help each other get dressed.

We are practising the play.

The play is tomorrow. We are practising it today. First we practise the songs.

Then we practise the dances.
My teacher shows us what to
do. My friends and I are parts
of a flower.

Today is the day of the play.
Our parents have arrived.
It is time for us to come in.

The play is starting.

The play is starting. We do our dance in the middle of the floor. We show how a flower opens in Spring.

It is fun.

I am very nervous but it is fun too. I don't forget the words of my poem.

Dad is filming me.

I can see my Mum and Dad in
the audience. Dad is filming
our play.

The play is over.

The play is over. We all have to bow. Everybody is clapping.

Mum and Dad are very proud.

My Mum and Dad loved our play.
They are very proud. Perhaps I'll
be an actor when I grow up!

Index

actor 19
audience 17

classroom 6
costumes 11

Dad 17, 19
dances 13
decorations 10

Mum 9, 17, 19

parents 14
play 7, 12, 14, 15, 18
poem 9, 16
practising 12, 13

scenery 8
songs 12
Spring 6, 7, 8, 15

teacher 7, 13

Notes to Parents and Teachers

Many children like nothing better than showing-off in front of an audience but for some performing in a play can be very stressful. Shy children hate to be the centre of attention and often find speaking to more than one person an ordeal. To them, standing on a stage and performing, or speaking on their own to a crowd, will be terrifying.

Parents can help to prepare children for plays and public events by encouraging them to perform in front of relatives and friends from an early age. If they are uncomfortable with this, care should be taken to include them in group scenes led by more confident children, rather than expect them to perform alone. Teachers can help by being sensitive to the needs and ability of each child.

A child may not be able to sleep the night before the play and may even be physically sick. No child should be forced to perform if it worries them this much. During the play children may 'freeze' or burst into tears. Teachers or parents should be at hand to reassure if this should happen. Above all, it should be remembered that a play is a happy, social event, and as long as children enjoy themselves it really does not matter if they forget their lines or do the wrong thing.

• If a child is too shy to perform, do not force the issue.

• Parents should be calm and supportive when helping children learn lines and prepare for their part.

• If a child falters during the performance, console them with instances of your own failures in life and try to help them move on.

• Remember to emphasise the excitement and fun of a play rather than what can go wrong.